*When you're in the company of angels,
things are always looking up.*

— Douglas Pagels

May You Always Have an

Angel

by Your Side

A Blue Mountain Arts® Collection

Edited by Douglas Pagels

Blue Mountain Press™

SPS Studios, Inc., Boulder, Colorado

Library of Congress Catalog Card Number: 00-012530
ISBN: 0-88396-590-9

Acknowledgments appear on page 64. The poem "May You Always Have an Angel by Your Side," written by Douglas Pagels, was originally published under a pseudonym with a name borrowed from his family tree. This book is dedicated to his extended family and his close friends.

Scripture quotation marked "NASB" is taken from the New American Standard Bible®. Copyright © The Lockman Foundation 1960, 1962, 1963, 1968, 1971, 1972, 1973, 1975, 1977, 1995. Scripture quotation marked "NKJV" is taken from the New King James Version. Copyright © 1982 by Thomas Nelson, Inc. Used by permission. All rights reserved.

Certain trademarks are used under license.

Manufactured in China
Third Printing in hardcover: December, 2001

This book is printed on fine quality, laid embossed, 80 lb. paper. This paper has been specially produced to be acid free (neutral pH) and contains no groundwood or unbleached pulp. It conforms with all the requirements of the American National Standards Institute, Inc., so as to ensure that this book will last and be enjoyed by future generations.

 This book is printed on recycled paper.

Library of Congress Cataloging-in-Publication Data

May you always have an angel by your side / edited by Douglas Pagels.
    p. cm.
  ISBN 0-88396-590-9 (alk. paper)
  ISBN 0-88396-584-4 (pbk : alk. paper)
  1. Angels—Quotations, maxims, etc. I. Pagels, Douglas.
  PN6084.A55 M39 2001
  291.2'15—dc21

00-012530
CIP

SPS Studios, Inc.

P.O. Box 4549, Boulder, Colorado 80306

Contents

(Authors listed in order of first appearance)

May You Always Have
an Angel by Your Side

May you always have an angel by your side •
Watching out for you in all the things you do •
Reminding you to keep believing in brighter days •
Finding ways for your wishes and dreams to
come true • Giving you hope that is as certain
as the sun • Giving you the strength of serenity
as your guide • May you always have love and
comfort and courage...

And may you always have an angel by your side • Someone there to catch you if you fall • Encouraging your dreams • Inspiring your happiness • Holding your hand and helping you through it all • In all of our days, our lives are always changing • Tears come along as well as smiles • Along the roads you travel, may the miles be a thousand times more lovely than lonely...

May they give you gifts that never, ever end:
someone wonderful to love and a dear friend
in whom you can confide ✦ May you have
rainbows after every storm ✦ May you have
hopes to keep you warm ✦

✦ And may you always have an angel
by your side ✦

— Douglas Pagels

Angels come to help and guide us in as many guises as there are people who need their assistance. Sometimes we see their ethereal, heavenly shadow, bright with light and radiance. Sometimes we only feel their nearness or hear their whisper. And sometimes they look no different from ourselves — until, their work done, they leave suddenly, quietly, with only a hint of halo or a wisp of wing behind to make us wonder.

— Eileen Elias Freeman

No one has to look very far to find proof
of an angel.... I've discovered that rather than
few and far between, angel encounters are
happening all around us and that very normal
people everywhere have been touched by
something or someone that has left them
with tremendous faith.

— Karen Goldman

Individual guardian, guiding angels
attend at least some of our ways and
hover protectively over our lives.

— Billy Graham

Everyone, no matter how humble he may be, has
angels to watch over him. They are heavenly, pure and
splendid, and yet they have been given us to keep us
company on our way; they have been given the task of
keeping careful watch over you.

— Pope Pius XII

Learn all you can about angels.
It's a form of higher education.

— Douglas Pagels

Angels exist in almost every culture and religion.
Not only do people of various social, cultural, and
economic backgrounds believe in angels, many of
them have had angelic experiences. The different
cultures may not always categorize them as angels,
but they do believe in real spirits that guard and
aid people in times of need.

— Constance Victoria Briggs

Angels appear in classical myth and philosophy,
in the vision of Shamans, in Hinduism, Buddhism,
Taoism, Zoroastrianism, and Islam, as well as in
Judaism and Christianity. In all traditions, angels
serve as messengers of God and are said to hover
between heaven and earth.

— Gail Harvey

Angels, like parables and fine poetry, speak in many layers of meaning and mystery, trying to express the inexpressible. If we ignore them, our lives are the poorer.

— Archbishop Desmond Tutu

The Language of Angels

In many traditions angels are involved with language: with creation stories, the workings of the universe, in music, chants, poetry and prayer, in the repositories of meaning, memories, and hope.

All those things with wings... dances of words... all are bound to tales of angels. They are gifts, moments, and notes grounded in eternity. The Sufi believe that each of the letters of the Arabic alphabet is ruled by an angel. Words, inner meanings, and interpretations are the domain of angels. In fact, the word for "angel" among the Sufis is the same as their word for icon — a window for the soul into the world beyond the veils that barely separate us from the divine.

— Megan McKenna

Angel
Blessings

Behold,
I am going
to send an angel
before you
to guard you
along the way.

— Exodus 23:20 (NASB)

May your days
all be blessed
with the presence
of an angel
watching over
you.

— Douglas Pagels

The delight of the wisdom of the angels
is to communicate to others what they know.

— Emanuel Swedenborg

Writ in the climate of heaven,
in the language spoken by angels.

— Henry Wadsworth Longfellow

What language do angels use?

The essence of the angels who come to us is the
ability to communicate perfectly with us, to convey
their messages clearly and unambiguously. How do
they do this?

It is clear from the experiences of many people who
have been touched by angels that they communicate
spiritually or telepathically — mind speaking to mind,
without the intermediary of a voice....

Whatever their means of communication among
themselves, it cannot be in language such as we use.
But when they touch us with their presence, they
communicate flawlessly.

— Eileen Elias Freeman

And Angel Voices Say...

The pure, the bright, the beautiful
That stirred our hearts in youth;
The impulses to wordless prayer,
The streams of love and truth;
The longing after something lost,
The spirit's yearning cry;
The striving after better hopes —
    These things can never die.

The timid hand stretched forth to aid
    A brother in his need;
A kindly word in grief's dark hour
    That proves a friend indeed;
The plea for mercy softly breathed
    When justice threatens high;
The sorrow of a contrite heart —
    These things shall never die.

Let nothing pass, for every hand
    Must find some work to do;
Lose not a chance to waken love;
    Be firm and just and true;
So shall a light that cannot fade
    Beam on thee from on high,
And angel voices say to thee —
    "These things shall never die."

— Charles Dickens

Out of every earth day,
make a little bit
of heaven.

— Ella Wheeler Wilcox

A Little Angelic Wisdom
to Carry with You Through the Day

Each day brings with it the miracle of a new beginning. Many of the moments ahead will be marvelously disguised as ordinary days, but each one of us has the chance to make something extraordinary out of them.

Remember that there is an enduring worth to every positive step you take, that the good decisions you make will come back to bless you, and that your angels will make sure that any clouds really do have a silver lining.

Have an absolutely wonderful day today!
Rise and shine...

And keep on rising.
And keep on shining.

— Douglas Pagels

We Never Know How High

We never know how high we are
  Till we are called to rise;
And then, if we are true to plan,
  Our statures touch the skies.

— Emily Dickinson

No limits are set to the ascent of man, and to each and every one the highest stands open. Here it is only your personal choice that decides.

Man is a ladder placed on the earth and the top of it touches heaven. And all his movements and doings and words leave traces in the upper world.

— Hasidic Saying

When we ask our angels to pray for us, we can be sure we have friends in the highest places.

— Eileen Elias Freeman

Angels are... the bridge between heaven and earth.

— Megan McKenna

The very presence of an angel is
a communication. Even when an
angel crosses our path in silence,
God has said to us, "I am here.
I am present in your life."

— Tobias Palmer

The soul at its highest is found like God,
but an angel gives a closer idea of Him.
That is all an angel is:
an idea of God.

— Johannes Meister Eckhart

Count always your highest moments
your truest moments.

— Phillips Brooks

When you are lonely or frightened, talk to your guardian angel. You can do it out loud, or inside your head — your angel can hear you whenever you speak. Ask your angel to be near you, to put his or her hand on your shoulder, to give you courage and protect you.

At other times, just enjoy the company of angels. And ask God to let you know more about these wonderful beings.

— Joan Wester Anderson

Sweet souls around us watch us still,
    Press nearer to our side;
Into our thoughts, into our prayers,
    With gentle helpings glide.

— Harriet Beecher Stowe

The vision of the angels
works softly and peaceably,
awakening joy and exultation.

— St. Athanasius

I believe that angels resort to drama only when
necessary, in order to break through our barriers
of consciousness. Once they have broken through,
they can commune with us on more subtle planes....

In fact, the angels would prefer not to use a heavy
hand. They would rather not crash about in the
material world. They would much rather have us
attune ourselves to the frequencies of a higher
consciousness, to the true music of our souls. When
we do that, as we listen carefully, we can hear...
their songs of guidance.

— Rosemary Ellen Guiley

Their miraculous activities are... accomplished in a manner so unobtrusive and so subtle that mortals are ignorant of their presence.

— Matthew Bunson

How to Explain?

We look at it and we do not see it;
Its name is the invisible.
We listen to it and do not hear it;
Its name is the inaudible.
We touch it and do not find it;
Its name is the subtle.

— Lao-Tzu

The best and most beautiful things in the world cannot be seen or even touched. They must be felt with the heart.

— Helen Keller

It is only with the heart that one can see rightly;
what is essential is invisible to the eye.

— Antoine de Saint-Exupéry

Make yourself familiar with angels, and behold
them frequently in spirit; for, without being seen,
they are present with you.

— St. Francis de Sales

The longer I live, the more my mind dwells upon the
beauty and the wonder of the world. I hardly know
which feeling leads: wonderment or admiration.

— John Burroughs

The larger the island of knowledge,
the longer the shoreline of wonder.

— Ralph W. Sockman

To be surprised, to wonder,
is to begin to understand.

— José Ortega y Gasset

All I have seen
teaches me to
trust the Creator
for all I have not seen.

— Ralph Waldo Emerson

Blessed are they that have not seen,
and yet have believed.

— John 20:29 (KJV)

Angels do not always make direct appearances....
Even when the landscape seems unoccupied by
angels, their presence can be felt. They have
flown, subtly but unmistakably, into the very
texture of ordinary life.

— Harriet Scott Chessman

It is to those who perceive... the poets,
the artists, and seekers for meaning,
that the angel makes himself known.

— Theodora Ward

Eventually you will come to your own
unique understanding about angels and
what they mean to you.

— David Connolly

There have been times when I have fallen
asleep in tears; but in my dreams the most
charming forms have come to cheer me,
and I have risen fresh and joyful.

— Johann Wolfgang von Goethe

Keep thou thy dreams — the tissue of all wings
    Is woven first from them; from dreams are made
The precious and imperishable things,
    Whose loveliness lives on, and does not fade.

— Virna Sheard

Angels... come as visions, voices, dreams, coincidences,
and intuition, the whisper of knowledge at your ear.
They come as animals or other people, or as a wash of
peace in an ailing heart. Sometimes a stranger may come
up and give you just the information or assistance you
need. Sometimes you yourself are used as an angel, for
a moment, either knowingly or not, speaking words you
did not know you knew.

But sometimes these beings come as angels, in the very
form that artists show — as beings of light, both with and
without wings.

— Sophy Burnham

I swear to you there are
divine things more beautiful
than words can tell.

— Walt Whitman

Angels are... divine, they are pure, they are powerful, they are beautiful, they are holy.

— David Connolly

Without fail, the angels answer the prayers and calls of all humanity... and the answer will come, according to our willingness to accept it.

— Patricia Diane Cota-Robles

When it seems
hardest to pray,
pray hardest.

— Hugh Black

If the only prayer you say in
your whole life is "Thank you,"
that would suffice.

— Johannes Meister Eckhart

Make friends with the angels.

— St. Augustine

Angels are... awesome beings deserving of great respect.

— Rosemary Ellen Guiley

We are like children, who stand in need of masters to enlighten us and direct us, and God has provided for this by appointing his angels to be our teachers and guides.

— St. Thomas Aquinas

O Guardian Angel, cover me with thy wing;
O Friend, illumine my path. Direct my
footsteps and be my protection,
just for today.

— St. Therese of Lisieux

I will not wish thee riches nor the glow of
greatness, but that wherever thou go
some weary heart shall gladden at thy smile,
or shadowed life know sunshine for a while.

And so thy path shall be a track of light,
    like angels' footsteps
        passing through the night.

— Inscription from a church
in Upwaltham, England

The farther we go along the path of God,
the more angels we shall encounter.

— H. C. Moolenburgh

All the way to heaven
is heaven.

— St. Catherine of Siena

For every angel fluttering through the skies,
there is a divine counterpart here on earth.
Each of us has a golden celestial self just
waiting to be awakened. Allow the angel
within you to emerge in expressions of
loving thoughts, and kindnesses.

— Liesl Vazquez

What is it like to come close to an angel, or to
listen to angelic tappings and whisperings,
advice and prophecy?

Angels can become astonishingly human
companions, just as humans — in their mystery
and their splendid otherness — can become
astonishingly angel-like. Intervening in human
lives, such angels have the power to help
people change their life-stories.

— Harriet Scott Chessman

Angel stories touch our innermost nature as if
with a magic wand, awakening all our brightest
hopes, our unsung dreams and wishes, and
washing clean our very souls.

— Karen Goldman

My soul is awakened, my spirit is soaring
And carried aloft on the wings of the breeze.

— Anne Brontë

With angel wings thy soul shall mount
To bliss unseen by eye.

— Anne Bradstreet

You Can Be an Angel, Too

In what specific ways can someone "be an angel" and serve?... You can be an angel by saying thanks to God for all the blessings in your life. Tell people that you are thankful to them and for all that they do for you.... You can be an angel by being true to your own truth and ideals. Angels touch us with their warmth. You can be an angel by touching and hugging someone, and sharing your warmth.... The angels uplift and inspire us to recognize our true divinity. You, too, can be an angel by inspiring someone with encouragement.

The angels are ministering spirits. They minister to our needs by bringing us messages of hope and joy. By writing a letter of joy or sending a card of hope to someone who needs it, you can be an angel, too....

Angels give us unexpected blessings, and you can be an angel by providing someone with a surprise when that person needs it most.... Angels are always ready to lighten our load in life by helping us carry the weight of our responsibilities and problems. You can be an angel whenever you say to someone who may be feeling overworked or overwhelmed, "Let me take care of you."

We might look at our lives and ask, "What can I give away today to someone?" If you don't have an abundance of money or material items to share, you can share your smile, your laughter, share your time, your energy, and your caring heart. Angels are interested in everything we do, so in order to qualify as an earth angel, you need to be interested in others.

— Jane M. Howard

You should remember that though another may have
more money, beauty, and brains than you, when
it comes to the rarer spiritual values such as charity,
self-sacrifice, honor, and nobility of heart, you have
an equal chance with everyone to be the most beloved
and honored of all people.

— Archibald Rutledge

Be an angel to someone else whenever you can,
as a way of thanking God for the help your angel
has given you.

— Eileen Elias Freeman

If You Come Across an Angel

Every day, in the world around us, real-life angels are doing the things they do and bringing more smiles to the world around them.

Real-life angels build bridges instead of walls. They don't play hide-and-seek with the truth, and they don't have hidden agendas. They tend to be the only ones who understand what you're going through. If they sense that you're hurting, they do whatever they can to help you.

Real-life angels understand difficulties and always give the benefit of the doubt. They don't hold others up to standards they can't live by themselves. Real-life angels are what "inner beauty" is all about.

Real-life angels don't hold things against you; the only thing they hold... is you. They take your hand in theirs when you could use a little reassurance. They walk beside you when you could do with a little guidance and direction in your life. And they support you in your attempts to do what is right.

Real-life angels multiply your smiles and add to your integrity. If you come across an angel like this, you are one of the luckiest people of all.

If someone in your life is wonderfully like an angel to you, it's important to let them know. It's the nicest compliment you could ever give.

— Douglas Pagels

Everyone can be
an angel.

— Cindy Crawford

Do not forget to entertain strangers, for by so
doing some have unwittingly entertained angels.

— Hebrews 13:2 (NKJV)

What a piece of work is man, how noble in reason,
how infinite in faculties, in form and moving, how
express and admirable in action, how like an angel.

— William Shakespeare

I don't know what your destiny will be, but
one thing I do know: the only ones among
you who will be really happy are those who
have sought and found how to serve.

— Albert Schweitzer

If you help others, you will be helped; perhaps tomorrow, perhaps in one hundred years, but you will be helped.

— G. I. Gurdjieff

Imagine yourself to be serving the holiest of beings when you serve your fellows. Keep nothing back when you feel enlightened by love for a passing friend or moved to lend a hand. Take all the joy you can from your experiences with others. Let love come straight from your heart.

As aspiring angels ourselves, we feel love for our fellow beings, for creatures and children, for the wonders of nature, for teachers, students, and friends.

None of us have to be so special to help the angels or be helped by them. We just need a little bit of faith.

— Karen Goldman

Faith goes up the stairs
that love has made
and looks out of the windows
which hope has opened.

— Charles H. Spurgeon

I live in a very small house,
but my windows look out
on a very large world.

— Confucius

Outside the open window
The morning air is all awash with angels.

— Richard Wilbur

Look up with unquenchable faith
in something ever more about to be.

— Zane Grey

The reason birds fly, and we can't, is simply that they have perfect faith, for to have perfect faith is to have wings.

— Sir James M. Barrie

God has given you a spirit with wings on which to soar into the spacious firmament of Love and Freedom.

— Kahlil Gibran

On Wings of Our Own

Let us be like a bird for a moment perched
    On a frail branch while he sings;
Though he feels it bend, yet he sings his song,
    Knowing he has wings.

— Victor Hugo

The Little Angel with One Wing

When I first saw the little ceramic angel, she was on a sale counter near a pile of old books. The smile on the face of the little figurine was so enchanting I moved closer, only to discover with a pang that the little angel had only one wing.

No doubt this accounted for the fact that she was with the reduced-in-price articles in the antique shop. She still carried a red apple in one hand, and golden schoolbooks in the other, as if intent on learning.

So the little angel with one wing came home with me to my writing room. Sometimes when my dreams did not all turn out as expected, I looked at the smiling figure and thought how all of us lose one wing of hope occasionally. Could I keep on as did my little angel?

Children automatically gravitated to the little angel, fondling her and stroking the one good wing. Always they asked, "What happened to the other wing?" Sometimes together we would make up a story about the missing wing.

She had loaned the other wing to another angel who had a load. Or she forgot the wing one day when she was flying home through a snowstorm. Or she was saving the wing to use on a flight to the full moon through the starry sky.

One day two little girls came to admire the angel, and their combined delight proved too much for the little figurine. As they tried to hand her to each other, they dropped her to the floor, and there was a loud crash followed by crying: Both of them said through their tears, "We broke the angel. Now her other wing is gone."

It was true. The little angel lay on the floor with her second wing a few feet away. I gathered the little girls in my arms and said, "Well, neither of you is hurt, and I'm so glad you told me the truth about breaking the angel."

We picked up the little figure and the wing and went in search of my husband, who turned to his tube of glue. Gently he put the wing in place and by nightfall the angel was again smiling in her accustomed place.

My husband said, "It's too bad you didn't have the other wing, for I could have put that back on for you, too, just as easily." But someone had long ago discarded that first wing.

Now the little angel with one wing constantly reminds me not to let go of the wings of hope.

If the first and best hope may be gone from our lives, surely there is one remaining wing, so life's dreams may be repaired. So may it always be with your dreams and mine, says the little angel with one wing, smiling from her shelf with her secret store of learning.

— Ruth C. Ikerman

A Wish, a Hope, a Prayer

I wish that every one of your days will dawn with a
sense of hope streaming in with the sunlight, a sense
of strength woven into the winds, and as many things
to be thankful for as there are stars in the evening sky.

I hope that the distance between where you are and
where you want to be grows shorter every day. I'll
never stop wishing that your journey through this
world will be touched by kindness, inspired by wisdom,
graced with understanding, and kept safe from all
harm. I hope you have a charmed existence, and that
your heart will always be an open window to a joy so
lasting and deep.

And I pray that you will always have an angel
watching over you, there to trace on your
wonderful face a smile that
you can keep.

— Douglas Pagels

Any man who does not believe in miracles
is not a realist.

— David Ben Gurion

As to me, I know of
nothing else but miracles.

— Walt Whitman

There is an unmistakable and profound reason why
every culture, every religion, every nation down
through the ages and in every part of the world
extols angels as fit representations of man's highest
conception of love and goodwill. They affect our
highest senses, inspire our noblest thoughts, reflect
our greatest aspirations.

— Karen Goldman

Angels have always been with us, in every time and culture. Ever since we emerged from the dim, distant past there have been records and representations of another race of beings who share this world with us. In pictograms and paintings, poetry and children's stories, our ancestors down through the ages have tried to pass on what they knew about these beings.

In the last few hundred years we have come to believe that something is real only if we can see it through a microscope or telescope. But no telescope will ever be powerful enough to see into the angelic realms.

— Alma Daniel, Timothy Wyllie, and Andrew Ramer

Whoever it was who searched the heavens with a telescope and found no God would not have found the human mind if he had searched the brain with a microscope.

— George Santayana

The most beautiful thing we can experience is the miraculous.

— Albert Einstein

Every blade of grass has an angel
bending over it saying, "Grow, grow!"

— Jewish Proverb

The moment one gives close attention to anything,
even a blade of grass, it becomes a mysterious,
awesome, indescribably magnificent world in itself.

— Henry Miller

If we had keen vision and feeling of all ordinary
human life, it would be like hearing the grass grow
and the squirrel's heart beat and we should die of
that roar which lies on the other side of silence.

— George Eliot

How silently, how silently,
The wondrous gift is given.

— Phillips Brooks

If we only understood our divinity,
we would have larger faith.

— Orison Swett Marden

Awe enables us to perceive in the world
intimations of the divine; to sense in small
things the beginning of infinite significance,
to sense the ultimate in the common and the
simple; to feel in the rush of the passing the
stillness of the eternal.

— Abraham Joshua Heschel

The angels keep their ancient places;
Turn but a stone, and start a wing!
'Tis ye, 'tis your estranged faces,
That miss the many-splendoured thing.

— Francis Thompson

It is in rugged crisis, in unweariable endurance...
that the angel is shown.

— Ralph Waldo Emerson

Whenever you are having anxious moments in your life, turn your thoughts to the angels and ask for a blessing of protection. Let the angels assist you. They are always there to offer a shoulder or to help you carry your burden.

— Jane M. Howard

I don't believe that tragedies and difficulties happen because angels desert us. Angels are always with us. For reasons... which we may not always be able to fully comprehend, we must at times in our lives go through pain.... Whenever we are confronted with problems, angels are ready to help us cope.

Pain provides us with opportunities for tremendous spiritual growth. Angels are not empowered to make decisions for us about our life's plan. They can only intervene when necessary to help keep that plan on track. They also can provide a source of spiritual nourishment when we most need it.

— Rosemary Ellen Guiley

God allows us to experience the low points of life in order to teach us lessons we could not learn in any other way.

— C. S. Lewis

Passing beyond the teaching of the Angels, the soul goes on to the knowledge and understanding of things.

— Clement of Alexandria

The soul should always stand ajar, ready to welcome the ecstatic experience.

— Emily Dickinson

We are born for a higher destiny than that of earth; there is a realm where the rainbow never fades, where the stars will be spread before us like islands that slumber on the ocean, and where the beings that pass before us like shadows will stay in our presence forever.

— Edward Bulwer-Lytton

An Angel's Hand

The gloom of the world is but a shadow. Behind it,
and yet within our reach, is joy. There is radiance and
glory in darkness could we but see; and to see we
have only to look. Life is so generous a giver, but we,
judging its gifts by their covering, cast them away as
ugly, or heavy, or hard. Remove the covering and you
will find beneath it a living splendor woven of love,
by wisdom, with power. Welcome it, grasp it, and
you touch the angel's hand that brings it to you.

Everything that we call a trial, a sorrow, or a duty —
    believe me,
        that angel's hand is there.

— Ernest Temple Hargrove

I have closed the door on doubt.
I will go by what light I can find,
    And hold up my hands
        and reach them out.

— Irene Pettit McKeehan

As much of heaven is visible
as we have eyes to see.

— William Winter

We shall find peace. We shall hear the angels,
we shall see the sky sparkling with diamonds.

— Anton Chekhov

Somewhere there's an angel... just waiting in
the wings for you. Let your heart listen to the
comfort, the wisdom, and the wondrous things
your angel is hoping to bring you. Believe, and
receive this blessing... and know that if you do,
there will be times in your life when your serenity
is sweeter, your understanding is greater, and
your joys are simply
out of this world.

— Douglas Pagels

An Angel Prayer for You

As the sun wakes up the world with its new
hopes for happiness, may it shine on you
and bring you the bright and beautiful gift
that it so lovingly holds...
　　　the gift of this special day ✦

You have an angel whose wishes consist of
such wonderful things for you! ✦ May you
have a day whose moments unfold with
peace, with promise, with doors that open
on new beginnings, and with windows that
look out on a world filled with dreams
waiting to come true ✦

May today not only be a day of duty done
and life's little battles won; may it be a time
of joy, of laughter, of memories made and
faith renewed ✦ May it be a time when feelings
of closeness are sweetly conveyed, when
truths are spoken, when smiles appear, and
when you just know, warm within your heart,
that your angel is always near...

May today be a sweet success ◆ Not in the
form of furnishings and wealth, but in the
much more dear and valuable ways: good
friends, good feelings, good health ◆ May
you and the loved ones in the circle of your
life always know the treasure of togetherness ◆

May a gentle gladness remind you that there
is never too little time to strive or too little
strength to climb ◆ May your joys be everlasting,
and your beliefs stay steady and deep and true ◆

And as each day comes full circle, and the
quiet times of reflection bring an evening of
serenity, may a distant dream find you, and
lovingly remind you that you have an angel
who will always keep a close watch... over you ◆

— Douglas Pagels

Little by little the angels have brought me back out into the sunlight and surrounded my heart with the fresh air of living. My heart is alive now, because it knows it has angels.... They protect us in ways that no one can see. They offer us their love, kindness, and safety when no one else understands what we need. When we can't put two and two together, when we can't define the trouble. Angels will help us fit back in when we've completely lost our footing.

Angels will always take care of us.
They will never go away.

— Karen Goldman

ACKNOWLEDGMENTS

We gratefully acknowledge the permission granted by the following authors, publishers, and authors' representatives to reprint poems or excerpts from their publications.

Warner Books, Inc., for "Angels come to help…" and "The essence of the angels…" from TOUCHED BY ANGELS by Eileen Elias Freeman. Copyright © 1993 by Eileen Elias Freeman. And for "When we ask…" and "Be an angel…" from THE ANGELS' LITTLE INSTRUCTION BOOK by Eileen Elias Freeman. Copyright © 1994 by Eileen Elias Freeman. All rights reserved.

Simon & Schuster, for "No one has to look…," "Angel stories touch…," "Imagine yourself…," and "Little by little…" from ANGEL ENCOUNTERS: TRUE STORIES OF DIVINE INTERVENTION by Karen Goldman. Copyright © 1995 by Karen Goldman. And for "There is an unmistakable…" from THE ANGEL BOOK: A HANDBOOK FOR ASPIRING ANGELS by Karen Goldman. Copyright © 1988, 1992 by Karen Goldman. All rights reserved.

Word Publishing, Nashville, TN, for "Individual guardian…" from ANGELS by Billy Graham. Copyright © 1975, 1986, 1994, 1995 by Billy Graham. All rights reserved.

Plume, a division of Penguin Putnam Inc., for "Angels exist…" from THE ENCYCLOPEDIA OF ANGELS by Constance Victoria Briggs. Copyright © 1997 by Constance Victoria Briggs. All rights reserved.

Portland House, a Division of Random House, Inc., for "Angels appear…" by Gail Harvey from ON THE WINGS OF ANGELS, compiled by Gail Harvey. Copyright © 1993 by Random House Value Publishing, Inc. All rights reserved.

Lynn C. Franklin Associates, Ltd., for "Angels, like parables…" by Archbishop Desmond Tutu. All rights reserved.

Orbis Books for "In many traditions…" and "[Angels are]…the bridge between…" from ANGELS UNAWARES by Megan McKenna. Copyright © 1995 by Megan McKenna. All rights reserved.

HarperCollins Publishers, Inc., for "The very presence…" from AN ANGEL IN MY HOUSE by Tobias Palmer. Copyright © 1994 by Winston Weathers. All rights reserved.

Ballantine Books, a Division of Random House, Inc., for "When you are lonely…" from AN ANGEL TO WATCH OVER ME by Joan Wester Anderson. Copyright © 1994 by Joan Wester Anderson. And for "Angels do not always…" and "What is it like…" from LITERARY ANGELS by Harriet Scott Chessman. Copyright © 1994 by Harriet Scott Chessman. And for "Angels… come as visions…" from ANGEL LETTERS by Sophy Burnham. Copyright © 1991 by Sophy Burnham. And for "Angels have always…" from ASK YOUR ANGELS by Alma Daniel, Timothy Wyllie, and Andrew Ramer. Copyright © 1992 by Alma Daniel, Timothy Wyllie, and Andrew Ramer. All rights reserved.

Pocket Books, a division of Simon & Schuster, for "I believe that angels…," "[Angels are]…awesome beings…," and "I don't believe…" from ANGELS OF MERCY by Rosemary Ellen Guiley. Copyright © 1994 by Rosemary Ellen Guiley. All rights reserved.

Three Rivers Press, a division of Crown Publishers, Inc., for "Their miraculous activities…" from ANGELS A TO Z by Matthew Bunson. Copyright © 1996 by Matthew Bunson. All rights reserved.

Harcourt, Inc., for "It is only…" from THE LITTLE PRINCE by Antoine de Saint-Exupéry. Copyright © 1943, renewed 1971 by Harcourt, Inc. All rights reserved.

W. W. Norton & Company, Inc., for "To be surprised…" from THE REVOLT OF THE MASSES by José Ortega y Gasset. Copyright © 1932 by W. W. Norton & Company, Inc., renewed 1960 by Teresa Carey. All rights reserved.

Viking Penguin, a division of Penguin Putnam Inc., for "It is to those…" from MEN AND ANGELS by Theodora Ward. Copyright © 1969 by Theodora V. W. Ward. All rights reserved.

Perigee Books, a division of Penguin Putnam Inc., for "Eventually you will come…" and "[Angels are]…divine, they are pure…" from IN SEARCH OF ANGELS by David Connolly. Copyright © 1993 by David Connolly. All rights reserved.

The Edgar Cayce Foundation and A.R.E. Press for "Without fail…" by Patricia Diane Cota-Robles, and for "You Can Be an Angel, Too" and "Whenever you are having…" by Jane M. Howard from COMMUNE WITH THE ANGELS by Jane M. Howard. Copyright © 1992 by Jane M. Howard. All rights reserved.

Peter Pauper Press, Inc., for "For every angel…" from ANGELS IN OUR MIDST by Liesl Vazquez. Copyright © 1994 by Peter Pauper Press, Inc. All rights reserved.

Cindy Crawford and Wolf-Kasteler Publicists for "Everyone can be…" by Cindy Crawford. All rights reserved.

Rhena Schweitzer Miller for "I don't know…" by Albert Schweitzer. Copyright © by the Albert Schweitzer Foundation, Inc. All rights reserved.

Citadel Press, an imprint of Kensington Publishing Corporation, for "God has given…" from A SECOND TREASURY OF KAHLIL GIBRAN, translated by Anthony Ferris. Copyright © 1962 by Citadel Press. All rights reserved.

A careful effort has been made to trace the ownership of selections used in this anthology in order to obtain permission to reprint copyrighted materials and give proper credit to the copyright owners. If any error or omission has occurred, it is completely inadvertent, and we would like to make corrections in future editions provided that written notification is made to the publisher:

SPS STUDIOS, INC., P.O. Box 4549, Boulder, Colorado 80306.